The Lives We Actually Have

THE WORKBOOK

Disclaimer

The information in this workbook is intended to be a guide to help you find blessing in the midst of messiness, ordinary life, your unique self, grief, anger, doubt, tiredness, joy, humanity, and life itself. It is not a substitute for professional spiritual counseling, advice, diagnosis, or treatment. If you are struggling with significant spiritual challenges, please consult with a qualified spiritual counselor or therapist.

The author of this workbook is not a licensed spiritual counselor or therapist. The information and exercises in this workbook are based on her personal and professional experience, as well as her research on blessed living.

The author is not responsible for any negative outcomes that may result from the use of the information or exercises in this workbook. Please use your own judgment and discretion when deciding whether or not to engage in any of the exercises.

LESSONS IN THIS WORKBOOK:

Chapter 1: Blessed Are the Messy

Our messy lives are worthy of blessing.

Our lives, no matter how messy or imperfect they may seem, have inherent worthiness. It encourages us to recognize that the challenges, setbacks, and complexities we face are an integral part of the human experience. By acknowledging the worthiness of our messy lives, we can begin to appreciate the growth, resilience, and valuable lessons that emerge from these experiences.

We don't have to have perfect lives to be blessed.

Blessings are reserved only for those with perfect, trouble-free lives. It highlights the idea that imperfections, struggles, and challenges are not barriers to receiving blessings. Instead, they can be opportunities for personal growth and transformation. By understanding that imperfection is part of life, we can free ourselves from the unrealistic pursuit of perfection and find contentment and fulfillment in the present moment.

Gratitude is a powerful practice that can help us to find blessing in the midst of messiness.

Importance: Gratitude is a transformative practice that allows us to shift our focus from what's lacking or difficult to what we already have and appreciate. This takeaway underscores the power of gratitude as a tool for finding blessings, even in the midst of life's messiness. By cultivating a habit of gratitude, we can develop a more positive outlook, improve our mental and emotional well-being, and become more resilient in the face of challenges.

Blessing Acknowledgment: Write about a recent messy or challenging situation in your life. Acknowledge that this situation, despite its messiness, is worthy of blessing. Reflect on the lessons or growth opportunities it may offer.

_____

_____

_____

_____

_____

_____

_____

_____

_____

_____

_____

_____

_____

_____

_____

_____

_____

_____

_____

_____

_____

_____

_____

_____

_____

_____

_____

Blessing Inventory: Create a list of five messy aspects of your life that you may have previously overlooked or taken for granted. Write about why each of these areas is worthy of blessing and how they contribute to your personal growth.

_____

_____

_____

_____

_____

_____

_____

_____

_____

_____

_____

_____

_____

_____

_____

_____

_____

_____

_____

_____

_____

_____

_____

_____

Messy Moments Reflection: Recall a particularly messy or difficult moment from your past that you now see as a source of blessing or growth. Write about how your perspective on this situation has evolved and how it has influenced your life in positive ways.

_____

_____

_____

_____

_____

_____

_____

_____

_____

_____

_____

_____

_____

_____

_____

_____

_____

_____

_____

_____

_____

_____

_____

_____

_____

_____

_____

_____

_____

_____

Lesson 2:

We don't have to have perfect lives to be blessed.

Blessed Imperfections: Write a letter to your future self, acknowledging that your life will never be perfect, and that's okay. Express your hope for future blessings despite imperfections. Share your current aspirations and how you plan to embrace imperfection on your journey.

_____

_____

_____

_____

_____

_____

_____

_____

_____

_____

_____

_____

_____

_____

_____

_____

_____

_____

_____

_____

_____

_____

_____

_____

_____

_____

_____

_____

_____

Embracing Flaws: Make a list of three personal imperfections or flaws you've struggled with. Write about how these imperfections have shaped you and your experiences. Reflect on how you can use them as sources of blessing and growth.

Imperfect Blessing Journal: Create a section in your journal where you regularly record imperfect moments that bring blessings into your life. Write about the ways in which these moments have enriched your life and contributed to your personal development.

_____

_____

_____

_____

_____

_____

_____

_____

_____

_____

_____

_____

_____

_____

_____

_____

_____

_____

_____

_____

_____

_____

_____

_____

_____

_____

_____

_____

_____

Lesson 3:

Gratitude is a powerful practice that can help us to find blessing in the midst of messiness.

Daily Gratitude Practice: Commit to a daily gratitude practice for one week. Write down three things you're grateful for each day, even if they relate to messy or imperfect aspects of your life. Reflect on how this practice shifts your perspective and brings blessings into focus.

_____

_____

_____

_____

_____

_____

_____

_____

_____

_____

_____

_____

_____

_____

_____

_____

_____

_____

_____

_____

_____

_____

_____

_____

_____

_____

Gratitude for Challenges: Identify a current challenge or messiness in your life. Write about at least three aspects of this situation for which you can be grateful. Explore how gratitude can help you find blessings in the midst of difficulty.

Gratitude Rituals: Develop a gratitude ritual that you can incorporate into your daily or weekly routine. Write about the specific actions or practices you'll use to express gratitude regularly and how this practice enhances your awareness of blessings.

Chapter 2: Blessed Are the Ordinary

Our ordinary lives are worthy of blessing.

Highlights the intrinsic value and worthiness of everyday life, regardless of how mundane or routine it may seem. It encourages us to recognize that even in the ordinary moments, there are blessings to be found. By understanding the worthiness of our ordinary lives, we can experience a sense of gratitude, contentment, and fulfillment in the present moment, rather than constantly seeking extraordinary experiences.

We can find beauty and meaning in the everyday moments.

Underscores the idea that beauty and meaning can be discovered in the simplest and most commonplace aspects of life. It encourages us to shift our perspective and actively seek out the profound in the ordinary. By finding beauty and meaning in everyday moments, we can enhance our overall sense of fulfillment, purpose, and joy in our daily experiences.

It's important to slow down and savor the ordinary.

In a fast-paced world, this takeaway reminds us of the significance of slowing down and fully immersing ourselves in the present moment. It encourages mindfulness and presence in our daily lives. By savoring the ordinary, we not only deepen our appreciation for the small details of life but also reduce stress, enhance well-being, and foster a greater sense of connection with the world around us.

Ordinary Blessings Journal: Create a dedicated section in your journal to record everyday blessings. Write about three ordinary moments or aspects of your life that you are grateful for each day. Reflect on how acknowledging these everyday blessings enhances your sense of worthiness and contentment.

_____
_____
_____
_____
_____
_____
_____
_____
_____
_____
_____
_____
_____
_____
_____
_____
_____
_____
_____
_____
_____
_____
_____
_____
_____
_____
_____

Blessings in Routine: Identify a daily routine or activity in your life that you typically take for granted. Write about the significance of this ordinary activity and how it contributes to your well-being. Explore how recognizing the blessing in routine can shift your perspective.

Appreciating the Mundane: Choose a mundane or routine task that you usually rush through or find unremarkable. Write a detailed description of the process and the sensations associated with it. Reflect on how paying close attention to the ordinary can reveal its hidden beauty and value.

_____

_____

_____

_____

_____

_____

_____

_____

_____

_____

_____

_____

_____

_____

_____

_____

_____

_____

_____

_____

_____

_____

_____

_____

_____

Lesson 2:

We can find beauty and meaning in the everyday moments.

Everyday Beauty Inventory: Keep a running list of everyday moments or scenes that strike you as beautiful or meaningful. Write about the feelings and thoughts these moments evoke. Reflect on how actively seeking out beauty in the ordinary enriches your daily life.

_____
_____
_____
_____
_____
_____
_____
_____
_____
_____
_____
_____
_____
_____
_____
_____
_____
_____
_____
_____
_____
_____
_____
_____
_____
_____
_____

Meaningful Everyday Rituals: Describe a simple, daily ritual or habit that brings meaning to your life. It could be as ordinary as making a cup of tea in the morning. Write about why this ritual is significant and how it contributes to your sense of purpose and well-being.

_____

_____

_____

_____

_____

_____

_____

_____

_____

_____

_____

_____

_____

_____

_____

_____

_____

_____

_____

_____

_____

_____

_____

_____

_____

Mindful Observation: Choose an ordinary object or scene in your surroundings. Spend a few minutes observing it closely, paying attention to details you might normally overlook. Write about your observations and how this practice of mindful observation deepens your appreciation of the everyday.

_____

_____

_____

_____

_____

_____

_____

_____

_____

_____

_____

_____

_____

_____

_____

_____

_____

_____

_____

_____

_____

_____

_____

Lesson 3:

It's important to slow down and savor the ordinary.

Mindful Eating Practice: During your next meal, practice eating mindfully. Write about the sensory experiences of taste, texture, and aroma. Reflect on how this practice of savoring the ordinary act of eating impacts your enjoyment of the meal and overall mindfulness.

Ordinary Moments Mindfulness: Dedicate five minutes each day to a mindfulness exercise focused on an ordinary moment. Write about the sensations, thoughts, and emotions that arise during this exercise. Reflect on how this daily practice of slowing down enhances your awareness of the ordinary.

Nature Connection: Spend time in a natural setting, such as a park or garden. Engage in a slow, mindful walk, paying attention to the sights, sounds, and sensations around you. Write about your experience and how connecting with nature can serve as a reminder to slow down and savor the beauty in the ordinary.

Chapter 3: Blessed Are the Strange Ducks

Our unique personalities and quirks are worthy of blessing.

Emphasizes the inherent worthiness of our individuality, including our unique personalities, quirks, and idiosyncrasies. It encourages us to recognize that our differences are what make us valuable and interesting as individuals. By acknowledging the worthiness of our unique selves, we can cultivate self-acceptance and self-esteem, leading to a more authentic and fulfilling life.

We are all made in the image of God, and each of us has a unique gift to offer the world.

Highlights the belief that every individual possesses inherent value and is a reflection of divinity. It emphasizes that each person has a unique gift, talent, or contribution to offer the world. Recognizing this truth can inspire a sense of purpose and meaning in our lives, as well as encourage us to explore and share our unique gifts with others.

It's important to embrace our unique selves and to celebrate our differences.

In a world that often pressures individuals to conform or hide their uniqueness, this takeaway stresses the significance of embracing and celebrating our authentic selves. It encourages us to be proud of our differences and to express our individuality confidently. By doing so, we not only enhance our own well-being but also contribute to a more diverse, inclusive, and accepting society that values and celebrates the uniqueness of every individual.

Self-Appreciation Letters: Write a letter to yourself expressing appreciation for one of your unique personality traits or quirks. Reflect on how this trait has contributed positively to your life or the lives of others. Keep this letter as a reminder of your worthiness and uniqueness.

Quirky Traits Reflection: List three quirky or unique traits or habits you possess. Write about how each of these traits makes you stand out or brings joy to your life. Share a personal story or experience related to each trait that highlights its value.

_____

_____

_____

_____

_____

_____

_____

_____

_____

_____

_____

_____

_____

_____

_____

_____

_____

_____

_____

_____

_____

_____

_____

_____

_____

_____

_____

_____

Acceptance Affirmations: Create a set of positive affirmations that celebrate your uniqueness. Write these affirmations on sticky notes and place them in prominent locations where you'll see them daily. Practice saying these affirmations aloud to reinforce self-acceptance.

Lesson 2:

We are all made in the image of God, and each of us has a unique gift to offer the world.

Gifts and Talents Inventory: Reflect on your skills, talents, and passions. Write a list of three unique gifts or qualities you believe you possess. Consider how these gifts align with your values and the positive impact they can have on your life and the lives of others.

Gifts of Service: Identify a way in which you can use one of your unique gifts to serve others or make a positive contribution to your community. Write a plan outlining the specific actions you will take to share this gift. Reflect on how this act of service aligns with your belief in being made in the image of God.

_____

_____

_____

_____

_____

_____

_____

_____

_____

_____

_____

_____

_____

_____

_____

_____

_____

_____

_____

_____

_____

_____

_____

_____

Gift Sharing Reflection: Write about a recent experience where you shared one of your unique gifts with someone or a group. Describe the impact of this gift-sharing on both yourself and the recipients. Reflect on how embracing and sharing your unique gifts contributes to a sense of purpose and fulfillment.

Lesson 3:

It's important to embrace our unique selves and to celebrate our differences.

Self-Discovery Journal: Dedicate a section in your journal to self-discovery. Write about one aspect of your uniqueness each day for a week, focusing on personality traits, quirks, or experiences that set you apart. Reflect on how embracing these differences can lead to greater self-acceptance.

Unique Others Celebration: Choose a friend, family member, or colleague and write them a heartfelt letter celebrating their unique qualities and contributions. Share specific instances where their uniqueness has made a positive impact. Reflect on how celebrating others' differences can foster stronger relationships.

_____

_____

_____

_____

_____

_____

_____

_____

_____

_____

_____

_____

_____

_____

_____

_____

_____

_____

_____

_____

_____

_____

_____

_____

Community Diversity Exploration: Explore the diversity within your community or neighborhood. Write about the unique qualities, cultures, or traditions of different individuals or groups you encounter. Reflect on the importance of celebrating this diversity and how it enriches your community.

_____

_____

_____

_____

_____

_____

_____

_____

_____

_____

_____

_____

_____

_____

_____

_____

_____

_____

_____

_____

_____

_____

_____

Chapter 4: Blessed Are the Grieving

Grief is a normal and healthy response to loss.

Importance: This emphasizes the normalcy and healthiness of grieving when we experience loss. It is important because it validates the natural emotional response that accompanies loss, whether it's the loss of a loved one, a job, a relationship, or any significant change. Recognizing grief as normal helps individuals understand that their feelings are valid and not something to be ashamed of. It allows people to process their emotions, ultimately aiding in the healing process.

We are not alone in our grief.

Grief can often feel isolating and lonely, making it crucial to acknowledge that others share in this universal experience. This takeaway highlights the importance of seeking support from friends, family, or support groups during times of grief. It reminds individuals that they are not the only ones going through this journey and that there is a sense of collective empathy and understanding. Knowing you are not alone can provide comfort and reduce feelings of isolation.

God is with us in our grief, and he offers us hope and comfort.

This brings spirituality and faith into the grieving process. It emphasizes that, for those who believe in a higher power or have a spiritual connection, there is a source of hope and comfort available. Recognizing the presence of God or a higher power can provide solace and strength during challenging times. It reinforces the idea that there is a source of support beyond human connections and encourages individuals to turn to their faith for healing and comfort.

Personal Grief Timeline: Create a timeline of significant losses or grief experiences in your life. Write a brief description of each event, including how you initially responded to the loss. Reflect on how your understanding of grief has evolved over time and how it has contributed to your healing process.

Grief Expression Letters: Write a series of letters to individuals who have experienced a significant loss. Share your empathy and understanding of their grief journey. Reflect on how acknowledging grief as a normal response can help others feel validated and supported in their grief.

_____

_____

_____

_____

_____

_____

_____

_____

_____

_____

_____

_____

_____

_____

_____

_____

_____

_____

_____

_____

_____

_____

_____

Grief Reflections Journal: Dedicate a section in your journal to reflect on your own grief experiences. Write about your emotional responses, coping mechanisms, and any lessons learned from each experience. Consider how recognizing grief as a normal and healthy response has influenced your ability to navigate loss.

Lesson 2:

We are not alone in our grief.

Grief Support Network Map: Create a visual representation of your support network during times of grief. Write down the names of family members, friends, or support groups that have been there for you during difficult times. Reflect on the significance of these connections and how they have helped you feel less alone in your grief.

Empathy Letters: Write a letter to someone you know who is currently grieving or has recently experienced a loss. Share your empathy and offer your support. Reflect on how reaching out to others in their grief can strengthen your own sense of connection and community.

_____

_____

_____

_____

_____

_____

_____

_____

_____

_____

_____

_____

_____

_____

_____

_____

_____

_____

_____

_____

_____

_____

_____

Grief Community Exploration: Research local grief support groups or online communities. Write about your experiences attending a support group meeting or engaging with an online community. Reflect on how connecting with others who share similar experiences has provided comfort and reduced feelings of isolation.

_____

_____

_____

_____

_____

_____

_____

_____

_____

_____

_____

_____

_____

_____

_____

_____

_____

_____

_____

_____

_____

_____

_____

_____

_____

_____

Lesson 3:

God is with us in our grief, and he offers us hope and comfort.

Faith Journal: Dedicate a section in your journal to explore your faith and spirituality in relation to grief. Write about your beliefs regarding God's presence during times of loss and how this belief has influenced your ability to find hope and comfort in your grief.

Hope and Comfort Affirmations: Create a set of affirmations that reflect your faith and provide hope and comfort during times of grief. Write these affirmations on index cards and place them in locations where you'll see them daily. Practice saying these affirmations as a source of strength.

Prayer and Meditation Practice: Incorporate a regular prayer or meditation practice into your routine. Write about your experiences with prayer or meditation during moments of grief. Reflect on how these practices have brought you a sense of God's presence and offered hope and comfort.

_____
_____
_____
_____
_____
_____
_____
_____
_____
_____
_____
_____
_____
_____
_____
_____
_____
_____
_____
_____
_____
_____
_____
_____
_____

Chapter 5: Blessed Are the Angry

Anger is a normal and healthy emotion.

This emphasizes that anger is a natural and common emotion that all humans experience. It's important because it helps normalize anger, reducing the stigma or shame often associated with it. Recognizing anger as a normal emotion allows individuals to validate their feelings and understand that anger, like other emotions, serves a purpose in our lives. It can motivate action, signal boundaries, and bring attention to important issues.

It's important to acknowledge our anger and to express it in healthy ways.

Acknowledging and expressing anger in healthy ways is crucial for emotional well-being. Suppressing or denying anger can lead to physical and emotional health issues, strained relationships, and unresolved conflicts. This takeaway underscores the significance of finding constructive outlets for anger, such as open communication, assertiveness, or creative expression. It encourages individuals to address their anger rather than bottling it up, leading to more positive and productive outcomes.

We can use our anger to fuel positive change in the world.

Anger has the potential to be a powerful catalyst for change when channeled constructively. This takeaway highlights that anger can be transformed into motivation for positive action, such as advocating for social justice, addressing personal boundaries, or standing up against injustice. It encourages individuals to harness the energy of their anger as a force for positive change rather than allowing it to become destructive or harmful.

Anger Journal: Dedicate a section in your journal to explore your own experiences with anger. Write about recent situations that made you angry, describing the events and your emotional responses. Reflect on how acknowledging anger as normal helps you better understand your emotional landscape.

Anger Awareness Practice: Set aside a specific time each day for an "anger check-in." Write down how you are feeling in terms of anger. Rate the intensity of your anger on a scale of 1 to 10 and briefly note the triggers. Reflect on how this practice of acknowledging and tracking your anger emotions contributes to emotional self-awareness.

Anger Expression Letters: Write a letter to someone you've been angry with in the past (whether you choose to send it or not). Express your feelings and thoughts about the situation and how it made you feel. Reflect on how the act of expressing your anger, even in writing, helps release the emotional tension.

Lesson 2:

It's important to acknowledge our anger and to express it in healthy ways.

Healthy Expression Strategies: Create a list of healthy ways to express anger when you feel it rising. Include actions like taking deep breaths, engaging in physical activity, or using "I" statements to communicate your feelings assertively. Write about times when you've used these strategies effectively and how they helped diffuse anger in a positive manner.

_____

_____

_____

_____

_____

_____

_____

_____

_____

_____

_____

_____

_____

_____

_____

_____

_____

_____

_____

_____

_____

_____

_____

_____

Anger Dialogue: Write a dialogue between yourself and an imaginary or real person with whom you've had a conflict that made you angry. Practice expressing your anger using healthy communication techniques. Reflect on how this exercise helps you find constructive ways to address anger-inducing situations.

Forgiveness and Release: Write a forgiveness letter to someone who has caused you anger or harm. Describe your feelings and experiences related to the situation, and express your willingness to let go of the anger and move toward healing. Reflect on how forgiveness and release can free you from the burden of anger.

Lesson 3:

We can use our anger to fuel positive change in the world.

Anger as Motivation: Reflect on a social or personal issue that makes you particularly angry or passionate. Write about how this anger can be channeled into positive action. Consider specific steps you can take to contribute to positive change related to this issue.

Anger-Fueled Advocacy Plan: Create a plan for getting involved in a cause or initiative that aligns with your values and the issues that make you angry. Write down the steps you can take to become an advocate or activist for change. Reflect on how channeling your anger into advocacy can lead to meaningful impact.

Community Connection: Research local or online groups or organizations that focus on issues you are passionate about. Write about your experiences joining or engaging with these communities. Reflect on how connecting with like-minded individuals who share your anger-driven motivations can lead to collective positive change.

Chapter 6: Blessed Are the Doubtful

Doubt is a normal part of the faith journey.

Importance: This takeaway underscores the idea that doubt is a common and expected aspect of one's spiritual or faith journey. It's important because it validates the experiences of individuals who grapple with doubt, reducing feelings of guilt or inadequacy. Recognizing doubt as normal allows individuals to explore their faith more authentically and openly, acknowledging that it's a natural part of the process.

We don't have to have all the answers.

Importance: This takeaway relieves the pressure of feeling like one must have all the answers or complete certainty in matters of faith or spirituality. It emphasizes that it's acceptable to have questions and uncertainties. Understanding that having all the answers is not a prerequisite for faith allows individuals to approach their spiritual journey with humility, curiosity, and a willingness to learn and grow.

God is with us in our doubt, and he invites us to explore our questions with honesty and openness.

Importance: This takeaway highlights the belief that God or a higher power is understanding and accepting of our doubts and questions. It encourages individuals to approach their faith with honesty and openness, rather than suppressing doubts. It fosters a sense of spiritual freedom and authenticity, allowing individuals to seek answers, engage in dialogue, and deepen their faith through the exploration of questions.

Doubt Journal: Dedicate a section in your journal specifically to explore your doubts about your faith or spirituality. Write about the doubts you've encountered recently or in the past, describing the specific questions or uncertainties. Reflect on how acknowledging doubt as normal helps you embrace your faith journey more authentically.

Doubt Discussion: Choose a trusted friend, family member, or mentor and engage in a conversation about your doubts. Write down the key points discussed and how this conversation made you feel. Reflect on how opening up about doubt can lead to greater understanding and support in your faith journey.

Doubt and Scripture: Select a passage or verse from a sacred text that addresses doubt or uncertainty. Write about your interpretation of this passage and how it relates to your own doubts. Reflect on the wisdom or guidance you find in these teachings.

Lesson 2:

We don't have to have all the answers.

Questions of Faith: Create a list of specific questions or uncertainties you have about your faith or spirituality. Write about why these questions are important to you and how they have influenced your journey. Reflect on the idea that not having all the answers is acceptable and even beneficial for personal growth.

Learning through Uncertainty: Write about a personal experience where you gained valuable insights or personal growth through grappling with uncertainty. Reflect on how the process of seeking answers and navigating uncertainty contributed to your spiritual development.

_____

_____

_____

_____

_____

_____

_____

_____

_____

_____

_____

_____

_____

_____

_____

_____

_____

_____

_____

_____

_____

_____

Embracing Mystery: Explore the concept of mystery in your faith or spiritual tradition. Write about how embracing the unknown and the mysteries of faith can be a source of inspiration and wonder. Reflect on how faith can coexist with questions and uncertainties.

Lesson 3:

God is with us in our doubt, and he invites us to explore our questions with honesty and openness.

Prayer of Honesty: Write a heartfelt prayer or meditation expressing your doubts, questions, and uncertainties to God or your higher power. Reflect on the experience of being open and honest in your spiritual communication and how it affects your sense of connection.

Seeking Guidance: Write about a time when you sought guidance or counsel from a spiritual leader or mentor regarding your doubts. Describe the advice or insights you received and how it impacted your perspective. Reflect on the importance of seeking support and wisdom when navigating doubt.

_____
_____
_____
_____
_____
_____
_____
_____
_____
_____
_____
_____
_____
_____
_____
_____
_____
_____
_____
_____
_____
_____
_____
_____
_____
_____

Community Exploration: Research local or online faith communities that encourage open dialogue and exploration of questions and doubts. Write about your experiences joining or engaging with these communities. Reflect on how a supportive community can help individuals feel less isolated in their faith journey.

Chapter 7: Blessed Are the Tired

It's okay to be tired.

This emphasizes the importance of acknowledging and accepting one's own fatigue and weariness. It's important because it validates the common human experience of feeling tired or overwhelmed. Recognizing that it's okay to be tired helps individuals let go of guilt or self-criticism and allows them to prioritize self-care and well-being.

We need to give ourselves permission to rest and recharge.

This highlights the necessity of self-care and rest in maintaining physical, emotional, and mental health. It emphasizes the importance of setting boundaries and allocating time for relaxation and rejuvenation. Recognizing the need to give oneself permission to rest promotes a healthier work-life balance and helps prevent burnout and exhaustion.

God is a God of rest, and he invites us to find Sabbath in our lives.

This brings spirituality and faith into the conversation about rest and rejuvenation. It underscores the belief that rest is not only acceptable but also a divine invitation. It encourages individuals to align their rest and rejuvenation practices with their spiritual beliefs and values, recognizing that taking time to recharge is in harmony with the idea of finding Sabbath and spiritual nourishment.

Tiredness Reflection: Set aside time in your journal to reflect on recent moments when you've felt tired physically, emotionally, or mentally. Describe the situations and your feelings. Write about any self-judgment or guilt you may have experienced regarding your tiredness. Reflect on how accepting that it's okay to be tired can alleviate these feelings.

Tiredness and Self-Compassion: Write a letter to yourself as if you were a friend or loved one who is feeling tired. Offer words of encouragement, understanding, and self-compassion. Reflect on how extending the same kindness to yourself as you would to others can help normalize tiredness and reduce self-criticism.

Tiredness Acceptance Affirmations: Create a set of affirmations related to tiredness, such as "I am allowed to feel tired," or "My tiredness does not define my worth." Write these affirmations on sticky notes and place them in visible locations as daily reminders. Reflect on how repeating these affirmations can help shift your perspective on tiredness.

Lesson 2:

We need to give ourselves permission to rest and recharge.

Rest and Recharge Plan: Write down a list of activities or practices that help you rest and recharge, such as reading, taking a nature walk, meditating, or spending time with loved ones. Schedule time for one of these activities in your upcoming week. Reflect on how prioritizing self-care activities contributes to your overall well-being.

Boundary Setting: Identify situations or commitments in your life that often leave you feeling exhausted or overwhelmed. Write about ways you can set boundaries or say "no" to some of these demands to create space for rest. Reflect on how implementing these boundaries can lead to a healthier balance in your life.

Daily Rest Ritual: Create a daily rest ritual that allows you to pause, even for a few minutes, and recharge during the day. Write about this ritual and how it makes you feel. Reflect on how small, intentional breaks can prevent burnout and help you stay more grounded.

_____

_____

_____

_____

_____

_____

_____

_____

_____

_____

_____

_____

_____

_____

_____

_____

_____

_____

_____

_____

_____

_____

_____

_____

_____

_____

_____

_____

Lesson 3:

God is a God of rest, and he invites us to find Sabbath in our lives.

Sabbath Reflection: Write about your understanding of the concept of Sabbath and how it aligns with your faith or spiritual beliefs. Reflect on times when you've experienced a sense of spiritual rest and rejuvenation. Write down specific practices or rituals that you associate with finding Sabbath in your life.

Sabbath Practice Planning: Create a plan for incorporating regular Sabbath practices into your life. Write about the specific activities or routines you will engage in to find spiritual rest. Reflect on how aligning your rest with your faith can deepen your connection with your spiritual beliefs.

Sharing Sabbath with Others: Write about the ways you can share the concept of Sabbath and the importance of rest with others in your community or faith group. Reflect on how encouraging others to prioritize rest aligns with your spiritual values and contributes to a sense of community well-being.

Chapter 8: Blessed Are the Joyful

Joyful Moments Journal: Set up a section in your journal to record moments of joy in your life, no matter how small they may seem. Describe the situations, people, or activities that brought you joy, and reflect on how these moments made you feel. Consider how recognizing joy as a gift from God enhances your gratitude.

Gratitude and Joy: Write about the connection between gratitude and joy. Reflect on how practicing gratitude can help you become more aware of the joy present in your life. Describe specific instances where gratitude deepened your experience of joy.

Joyful Prayers: Create a prayer or meditation focused on joy. Express your gratitude for the joy in your life and ask for guidance in recognizing and cultivating more joy. Reflect on how incorporating joy into your spiritual practice enriches your connection with God.

_____

_____

_____

_____

_____

_____

_____

_____

_____

_____

_____

_____

_____

_____

_____

_____

_____

_____

_____

_____

_____

_____

_____

_____

_____

Lesson 2:

We can find joy in the midst of even the most difficult circumstances.

Finding Joy in Challenges: Write about a challenging or difficult situation you've faced in the past and how you were able to find moments of joy or positivity within it. Reflect on the strategies or perspectives that helped you discover joy during adversity.

Joyful Resilience: Describe a personal experience where you demonstrated resilience and found joy despite difficult circumstances. Write about the emotions you felt during that time and how you were able to maintain a sense of hope and joy. Reflect on the resilience you possess and how it can be a source of ongoing joy.

Daily Joyful Reflection: Incorporate a daily practice of reflecting on one positive or joyful aspect of your day, no matter how challenging the overall circumstances may be. Write down your reflections each day and notice how this practice shifts your perspective on difficulties over time.

_____
_____
_____
_____
_____
_____
_____
_____
_____
_____
_____
_____
_____
_____
_____
_____
_____
_____
_____
_____
_____
_____
_____
_____
_____
_____
_____

Lesson 3:

Joy is contagious, and we can spread it to others by simply being joyful ourselves.

Spreading Joy through Acts of Kindness: Write a list of small acts of kindness you can perform to spread joy to others, such as sending an encouraging message, sharing a compliment, or offering assistance. Commit to performing one of these acts each day for a week and journal about the impact it has on both you and the recipients.

Joyful Presence: Reflect on the influence of your own joy on the people around you, whether it's in your family, workplace, or community. Write about specific instances where your joyful presence had a positive effect on others. Consider how you can intentionally bring more joy into your interactions.

_____
_____
_____
_____
_____
_____
_____
_____
_____
_____
_____
_____
_____
_____
_____
_____
_____
_____
_____
_____
_____
_____
_____
_____

Creating a Joyful Environment: Describe ways you can create a joyful and positive environment in your personal spaces, such as your home or workspace. Write about the changes you plan to make and how these changes can contribute to a more joyful atmosphere for yourself and those who share the space with you.

Chapter 9: Blessed Are the Human

Reflecting on Imperfections: Write about a recent mistake or imperfection you've experienced. Describe the situation and your feelings at the time. Reflect on how acknowledging your humanity and capacity for mistakes can reduce feelings of shame or self-criticism.

_____

_____

_____

_____

_____

_____

_____

_____

_____

_____

_____

_____

_____

_____

_____

_____

_____

_____

_____

_____

_____

_____

_____

_____

_____

_____

_____

_____

Embracing Vulnerability: Share a personal story of a mistake or vulnerability with someone you trust, either through conversation or a heartfelt letter. Write about the experience and the emotions it brought up. Reflect on how opening up about your imperfections can lead to deeper connections and understanding.

Accepting Imperfections: Create a list of affirmations or self-compassionate statements related to embracing your humanity and imperfections, such as "I am worthy of love and forgiveness despite my mistakes." Write these affirmations on sticky notes and place them in visible locations as daily reminders. Reflect on how repeating these affirmations can help shift your self-perception.

Lesson 2:

God loves us and forgives us for our mistakes.

Forgiveness Journal: Dedicate a section in your journal to explore the theme of forgiveness, both from God and from yourself. Write about times when you felt forgiven or extended forgiveness to others. Reflect on the sense of grace and love associated with forgiveness.

_____

_____

_____

_____

_____

_____

_____

_____

_____

_____

_____

_____

_____

_____

_____

_____

_____

_____

_____

_____

_____

_____

_____

_____

_____

_____

_____

_____

Prayer of Forgiveness: Write a prayer or meditation focused on seeking forgiveness from God for a specific mistake or wrongdoing. Express your remorse, ask for forgiveness, and commit to learning from the experience. Reflect on the healing and transformative power of forgiveness.

Letter of Self-Forgiveness: Write a heartfelt letter to yourself, addressing a specific mistake or regret. Practice self-forgiveness by acknowledging your humanity, expressing forgiveness, and affirming your commitment to personal growth. Reflect on how this act of self-forgiveness can bring emotional healing.

Lesson 3:

We can learn and grow from our mistakes.

Mistake Reflection and Growth Plan: Write about a significant mistake or failure you've experienced in your life. Describe the lessons you learned from this experience and how it contributed to your personal growth and development. Reflect on the idea that mistakes can be valuable teachers.

Turning Mistakes into Goals: Identify a specific area in your life where you'd like to improve or set a goal. Write about how the lessons from past mistakes can inform your goals and action plan. Reflect on how using mistakes as stepping stones can lead to more intentional growth.

Sharing Growth Stories: Share a story of a personal mistake or failure with someone you trust and respect, highlighting the growth and insights you gained from it. Write about the experience of sharing your journey of learning and growth and how it can inspire others to embrace their own mistakes as opportunities for growth.

Chapter 10: Blessed Are the Living

Life Gratitude List: Create a list of things in your life that you are grateful for, recognizing life as a precious gift. Write down specific experiences, relationships, or moments that make you appreciate the gift of life. Reflect on how acknowledging life as a gift enhances your sense of gratitude.

_____

_____

_____

_____

_____

_____

_____

_____

_____

_____

_____

_____

_____

_____

_____

_____

_____

_____

_____

_____

_____

_____

_____

_____

Life Reflections: Take a moment to reflect on significant milestones or turning points in your life. Write about the experiences that have shaped you, both positive and challenging. Consider how your life journey is a unique gift from God, and reflect on the lessons you've learned along the way.

_____

_____

_____

_____

_____

_____

_____

_____

_____

_____

_____

_____

_____

_____

_____

_____

_____

_____

_____

_____

_____

_____

_____

_____

_____

_____

Life Affirmations: Develop a set of affirmations or statements related to the gift of life, such as "I honor the gift of life by living it fully" or "I am grateful for the opportunities each day brings." Write these affirmations on sticky notes and place them in visible locations as daily reminders. Reflect on how repeating these affirmations can help you cherish life.

Lesson 2:

Each day is a blessing.

Daily Blessings Journal: Dedicate a section in your journal to record daily blessings, no matter how small they may seem. Write about positive moments, encounters, or achievements from each day. Reflect on how this practice shifts your perspective and helps you recognize the blessings in everyday life.

Mindful Living Practice: Choose a day to practice mindful living. Write about your experience of being fully present in each moment, whether it's during routine activities or special occasions. Reflect on how mindfulness enhances your awareness of daily blessings and the beauty of ordinary moments.

Daily Blessing Intentions: Start each day by setting an intention to notice and appreciate the blessings that come your way. Write down your intention and make a commitment to carry it throughout the day. Reflect on how setting this intention shapes your perception of daily life.

_____

_____

_____

_____

_____

_____

_____

_____

_____

_____

_____

_____

_____

_____

_____

_____

_____

_____

_____

_____

_____

_____

_____

_____

_____

Lesson 3:

We should make the most of the time we have been given.

Time Management Reflection: Reflect on your current approach to time management. Write about how you allocate your time and whether it aligns with your values and priorities. Consider areas where you can make adjustments to ensure you are making the most of the time you've been given.

Creating a Time Capsule: Imagine you are creating a time capsule that represents your life and the legacy you want to leave behind. Write about the items, memories, or values you would include in this capsule. Reflect on how this exercise can inspire you to make the most of your time and leave a meaningful legacy.

_____

_____

_____

_____

_____

_____

_____

_____

_____

_____

_____

_____

_____

_____

_____

_____

_____

_____

_____

_____

_____

_____

_____

Setting Daily Intentions: Start each day by setting one or two specific intentions for how you will make the most of your time. Write down your intentions and take note of the actions you take to fulfill them. Reflect on how setting daily intentions empowers you to live purposefully.

Made in the USA
Las Vegas, NV
04 November 2023

80197292R00069